A Children's Book About

BEING MESSY

Managing Editor: Ellen Klarberg
Copy Editor: Annette Gooch
Editorial Assistant: Lana Eberhard
Art Director: Jennifer Wiezel
Production Artist: Gail Miller
Illustration Designer: Bartholomew
Inking Artist: Rashida Tessler
Coloring Artist: Berenice Happé Iriks
Lettering Artist: Linda Hanney
Typographer: Communication Graphics

A Children's Book About

BEING MESSY

By Joy Berry

GROLIER ENTERPRISES CORP.

This book is about Annie.

Reading about Annie can help you understand and deal with **being messy.**

You are being messy when you
- spill food on your clothes or
- drop food on the furniture or floor.

You are being messy when you
- walk into clean areas with dirty feet,
- touch furniture or walls with dirty hands, or
- sit on furniture while wearing dirty clothes.

You are being messy when you do not put your trash and garbage in appropriate containers.

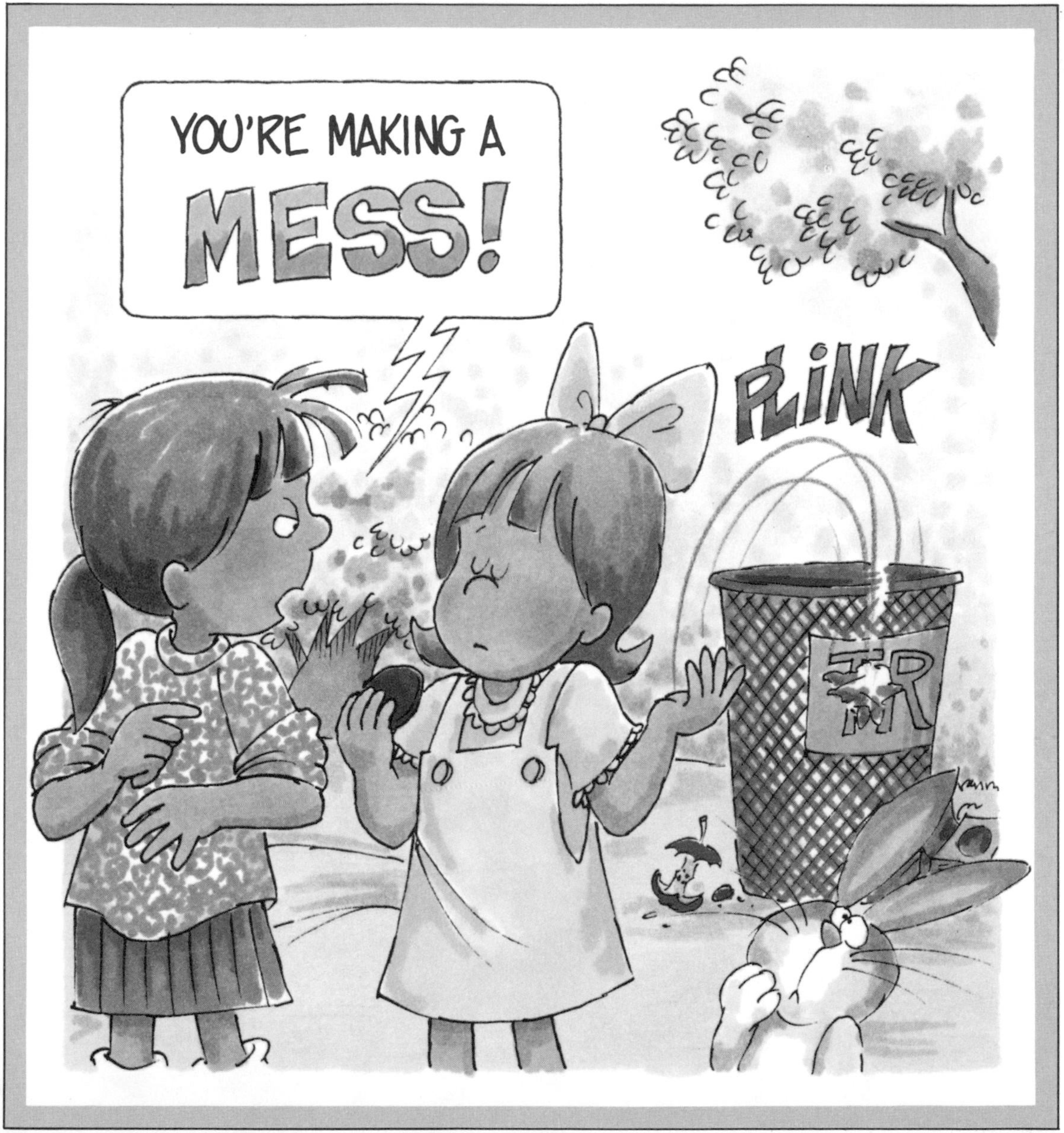
YOU'RE MAKING A MESS!
PLINK

You are being messy when you
- do not put things away after you use them,
- do not put things where they belong, or
- do not put things away neatly.

You are being messy when you are careless with things such as crayons, paints, pens, clay, or glue. You are being messy when you get things on your clothes or your surroundings.

A mess can be *displeasing*.

Most people enjoy cleanliness, order, and beauty. A mess is not clean. It is not orderly. It is not beautiful. A mess does not make people happy. It usually makes them unhappy.

A mess can be *frustrating*. People might become upset if they cannot find what they are looking for because
- it is hidden by clutter or
- it is not where it belongs.

A mess can be *destructive*.

- Your clothes and surroundings can be ruined by messy stains.
- Things that are left out can be damaged accidentally.
- Things that are not put away carefully can be ruined.

A mess can be *dangerous*.
- People can slip and possibly fall because of messy spills.
- People can trip over things that are out of place.

Messes can be
- displeasing,
- frustrating,
- destructive, and
- dangerous.

This is why you should not be messy.

An accident can cause a mess. You can avoid accidental messes by *being careful*.

There are things you can do to avoid messes.

To prevent a mess:
- Cover your clothes before you do something that might be messy. (Use a napkin, apron, or smock.)
- Protect the area where you are working by covering it with newspapers, an old sheet, or a tablecloth.

To prevent a mess:
- Keep yourself and your clothes as clean as possible.
- Wash your hands before you touch clean things.
- Get the dirt, mud, or sand off your feet before you walk into a clean area.

To prevent a mess:
- Do not litter. Put trash in a trash container. Put garbage in a garbage disposal or container.
- Put things away when you are finished using them. Put things away neatly where they belong.

You and the people around you will be
happier if you avoid being messy.